TOP BEACHES
OF THE WORLD

Traumhafte Strände - Reiseziele zum Träumen
Dream beaches and travel destinations

Herausgegeben von/ Edited by Robert Gabor

OIO

Published by: OIO Books, NewLevel Est., Schaanerstr.13, LI-9490 Vaduz
www.oiobooks.com

ISBN 978-3-03889-014-0

 Bibliographic information of the Liechtensteinische Landesbibliothek: The Liechtensteinische Landesbibliothek lists this publication in the National Bibliography of Liechtenstein; detailed bibliographic information can be found on the Internet at www.landesbibliothek.li.

Die Sehnsucht nach „unserem“ Traumstrand rührt vielleicht daher, dass wir Menschen als ehemalige Wesen des Meeres irgendwann einmal von dort herkamen und uns dann an Land weiterentwickelten. Hierbei muss man sich vor Augen führen, dass es sich bei etwa nur einem Prozent der weltweiten Küstenlinie um Sandstrände handelt. Dieser Band stellt einige der wohl allerschönsten Strände der Welt vor. Jene Strände, die man mit Fug und Recht als magische Sehnsuchtsorte bezeichnen darf. „Top Beaches of the World“ zeigt in grandiosen Bildern mehr als 80 der schönsten Strände unseres Planeten, ob groß oder klein, einsam oder belebt. Alle diese Orte sind von außergewöhnlichem Zauber. Destinationen aus der ganzen Welt, die zum Träumen einladen und die man in diesem Buch staunend mit den Augen bereisen kann. Paradiesische Strände, die es – gerade in Zeiten des Massentourismus – für kommende Generationen zu bewahren gilt.

The longing for "our" dream beach probably comes from the fact that we human beings are once creatures of the sea; we came from there long ago and went on to develop on the land. It should be borne in mind that only about one per cent of the world's coasts are sandy beaches. This book presents what are probably some of the loveliest beaches in the world. Beaches that can fully justifiably be described as magical places of deep desire. In a series of magnificent images, "Top beaches of the world" presents more than 80 of the loveliest beaches on our planet, both small and large, lonely and busy. All of these places possess an exceptional magic. Destinations from all over the world which make you dream, and which you can explore in this book with eyes open wide in amazement. Paradisiacal beaches which need to be protected for generations to come – especially in these times of mass tourism.

Der atemberaubendste Strand
The most breathtaking beach

Napali Coast/ Hawaii/ USA

Einfach nur majestätisch: Die berühmte Napali Coast auf der hawaiianischen Insel Kauai ist eine pazifische Schönheit. Weißer Sandstrand gesäumt von schroffen Klippen mit smaragdfarbenen Gipfeln.

Simply majestic: The famous Napali beach on the Hawaiian island of Kauai is a pacific beauty. White sandy beach bordered by steep cliffs with emerald colored peaks.

Einer gezackten Krone gleich, reiht die Napali Coast Gipfel an Gipfel. Jede Bergspitze ist dabei ein Höhepunkt für sich. Gesäumt von einem zauberhaften Sandstrand, ist die Küste eine wahre Glanzleistung der Natur.

Like a serrated crown, Napali beach is surrounded by a series of peaks. Every peak here is a high point for itself. The coast is bordered by a magical sandy beach, a truly brilliant work of art by nature.

Südseefeeling auf fast 30 Kilometern Länge. Ein weitgehend unberührter Garten Eden vor dessen Ufern man Schnorcheln und in Höhlen baden kann. Kauai wird wegen seiner üppigen Vegetation auch als die Garteninsel Hawaiis bezeichnet.

A South Seas feeling on almost 30 kilometers of length. A garden of Eden unchanged to a large extent, where you can swim from its banks and snorkel in caves. Kauai is also designated the garden island of Hawaii because of its opulent vegetation.

Die unheimlichste Strand
The very eerie beach
Skeleton Coast/ Namibia

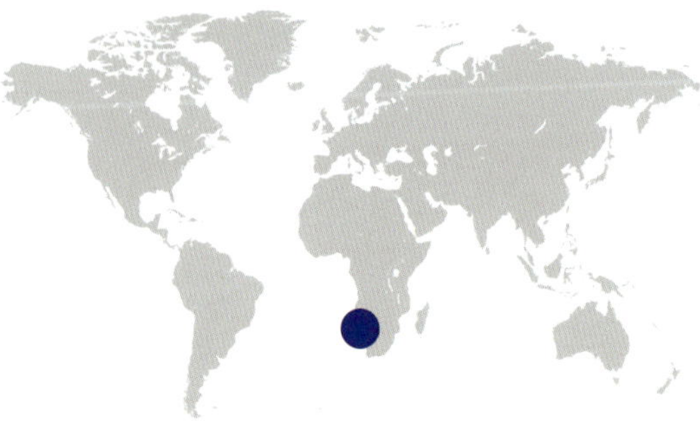

Hier, wo die Wüste Namib auf den Atlantik trifft, liegen an der Küste hunderte von Schiffswracks. Buschmänner nennen diese Küste „das Land, das Gott im Zorn erschuf" und portugiesische Seeleute bezeichneten sie als „das Tor zur Hölle". Auf dem Eingangstor zum Nationalpark sind überdimensional große Totenköpfe abgebildet.

Here, where the Namibia desert meets the Atlantic, hundreds of shipwrecks litter the coast. Bushmen call this coast "the country that God created in anger" and Portuguese sailors designated it "the gate to hell". On the entrance gate to the national park, over-sized death's-head skulls are pictured.

Schiffbrüchige, die sich von den an der Küste gestrandeten Wracks hatten retten können, hatten dennoch keine Überlebenschance, da sie in der unbesiedelten, extrem trockenen Küstenwüste elendig verdursteten. Der Name bezieht sich daher sowohl auf die Schiffs-„Skelette“, die echten Skelette der Gestrandeten, aber auch auf die zahlreichen Gerippe von an Land gespülten Walen.

Castaways who were able to save themselves from the beached wrecks, nevertheless had no chance of survival, since they were in an unsettled, extremely dry, coastal desert which was miserably arid. The name therefore refers both to the ship "skeletons" and to the genuine skeletons of the stranded sailors, however, also to the numerous skeletons of whales washed up on land.

Der aus der Antarktis kommende kalte Benguelastrom erzeugt ablandige Winde und ist die Ursache für die direkt am Strand beginnende Küstenwüste und den oft sehr dichten Nebel. Und genau dieser tödlichen Kombination von Nebel und Wüste verdankt die Skeleton Coast ihren Namen.

The cold Benguela current coming from Antarctica generates off-shore winds and is the cause for the coastal desert beginning directly on the beach and the often very thick mist. And it is exactly this fatal combination of mist and desert that gives the Skeleton Coast its name.

Der weicheste Strand
The softest beach
Ile aux Cerfs/ Mauritius

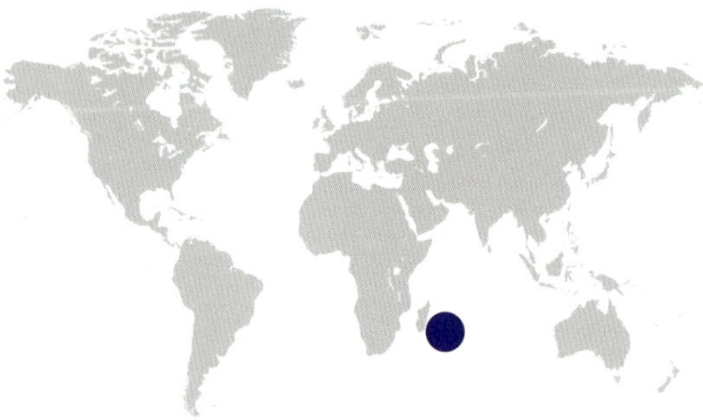

Die an der Ostküste von Mauritius gelegene, vorgelagerte Insel Ile aux Cerfs ist genau das, was sich Urlauber unter Mauritius vorstellen: türkisblaues Wasser und weiße Sandstrände. Durch die stete, leichte Strömung von Ebbe und Flut und das leicht abfallende Ufer entstand an diesem Kanal ein besonders weicher Strand. und sattgrüne Palmen. Die «Hirschinsel» blieb jedoch nicht lange ein Geheimtipp. So kommen jeden Tag zahlreiche Tagesausflügler, sowie die Gäste des Hotels Touessrok auf die Insel. Auch wenn es sich um keine einsame Insel mehr handelt, bleibt ein Ausflug auf das wunderschöne Eiland ein Muss für jeden Mauritius-Urlaub. Nach wie vor kommt die Ile aux Cerfs dem typischen Inseltraum sehr nahe.

The island Ile aux Cerfs located offshore on the east coast of Mauritius is exactly what holiday-makers imagine Mauritius to be: Turquoise-blue water and white sandy beaches.
An especially soft beach has been formed at this channel from the continuous, easy flow of high and low tides and the bank dropping off slightly. And voluptuously green palms. However «Stag Island» has not remained a secret for very long. Numerous daily excursions come every day, as well as visitors from the hotel Touessrok on the island. Even if it is not a lonely island any more, an excursion to this wonderful island remains a necessity for every Mauritius vacation. Ile aux Cerfs still comes very close to the typical island dream.

Der Strand mit den rundesten Felsen
The beach with the most rounded rocks

Koekohe Beach/Neuseeland

Nach Legenden der Maori sind die runden Moeraki Boulders Reste von Aalkörben, die vom Wrack des legendären Kanus Arai-te-uru an Land gespült wurden. In Wirklichkeit handelt es sich jedoch um kugelförmige Verwachsungen von Kristallen (Konkretionen), die von der Küstenerosion freigelegt wurden.

According to Maori legend, the round Moeraki Boulders are residues of eel baskets that were washed up on land from the wreck of the legendary canoe Arai-te-uru. In reality, however, it involves spherical intergrowths of crystals (concretions) which were exposed by coastal erosion.

Die Konkretionen der Moeraki Boulders sind mit einem Durchmesser von bis zu 2,2 Metern ungewöhnlich groß und liegen einzeln oder in Gruppen am Strand. Die Mehrzahl ist nahezu perfekt kugelförmig und daher eine touristische Sehenswürdigkeit.

The concretions of the Moeraki Boulders are unusually large, with a diameter of up to 2.2 meters, and are present on the beach separately or in groups. The majority are almost perfectly spherical and therefore a tourist sight.

Der Strand mit der größten Domkuppel
The beach with the largest dome
Praia de Benagil/Portugal

Am Strand von Benagil ist eine einzigartige Felshöhle der eigentliche Touristenmagnet. Man kann den vom Meer ausgespülten und als „Kathedrale" bekannten Hohlraum schwimmend oder per Boot erreichen man bei Ebbe den als "Kathedrale" bekannten, vom Meer ausgespülten Hohlraum. Er findet sich auf vielen Postkarten der Algarve.

On the beach of Benagil is a unique rock cave of the unique tourist magnet. You can reach the hollow space known as "Cathedral" by swimming or by boat. By swimming or by boat, at low tide you can reach the hollow space known as the "Cathedral" which has been formed by the sea.
It is illustrated on many postcards of the Algarve

Der symmetrischste Strand
The most symmetrical beach
Zlatni Rat Beach/Kroatien/Croatia

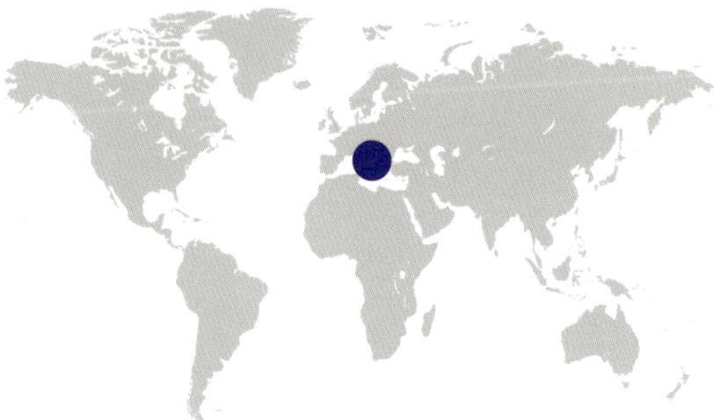

Das Goldene Horn (kroatisch Zlatni rat) ist einer der beliebtesten Strände Kroatiens. Er befindet sich auf der dalmatinischen Insel Brac und ist eigentlich zumeist sichelförmig, da er sich je nach Strömung hin und her bewegt. Wenn seine Spitze in der Mitte steht, ist er nahezu perfekt symmetrisch.

The Golden Horn (Croatian Zlatni rat) is one of the most popular beaches in Croatia. It is located on the Dalmatian island of Brac and is in fact mostly sickle-shaped, since it is moved back and forth according to the tide. When its peak is in the middle, it is almost perfectly symmetrical.

Der die meisten Inseln verbindende Strand
The beach connecting the most islands

Koh Nang Yuan/ Thailand

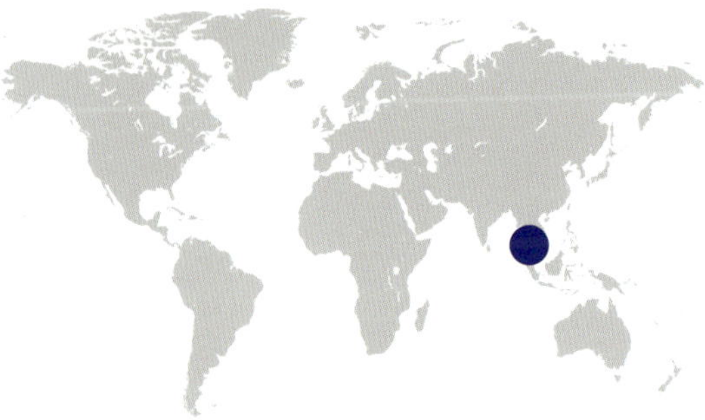

Der Aussichtspunkt der Insel Koh Nang Yuan bietet einen grandiosen Ausblick. Man kann bewundern, wie ein aus drei winzigen Inseln bestehender Mini-Archipel durch einen einzigen in drei Richtungen weisenden Strand verbunden wird.

The lookout point of the island of Koh Nang Yuan offers an overwhelming view. You can admire how a mini-archipelago, consisting of three tiny islands, is connected by a single beach pointing in three directions.

Der von den meisten Treppen gesäumte Strand
The beach lined with the most steps

Reynisfjara/Island

An der Südküste Islands erstreckt sich zwischen Dyrhólaey und dem Berg Reynisfjall der berühmteste schwarze Sandstrand der Insel – der Reynisfjara. Auffällig sind die gewaltigen Basaltsteinformationen direkt am Strand. Sie ragen wie riesige Treppen in den Himmel. Ein Ort voll wilder und dramatischer Schönheit.

On the south coast of Iceland, the most well-known black sandy beach of the island - the Reynisfjara - extends between Dyrhólaey and Reynisfjall mountain. The tremendous basalt stone formations occur directly on the beach. They jut out as gigantic stairways into the sky. A location full of wild and dramatic beauty.

Die beeindruckendsten weißen Kreidefelsen
The most impressive white chalk cliffs

Seven Sisters, East Sussex/England

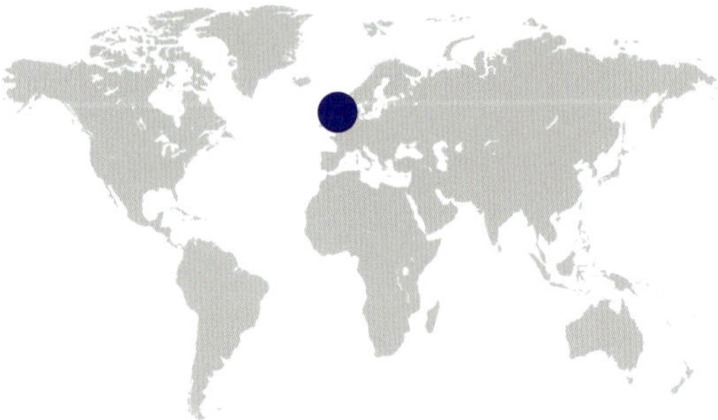

Als die „Sieben Schwestern“ wird die Küste zwischen Eastbourne und Seaford im Süden Englands bezeichnet. Bei diesen eindrucksvollen, gewaltig hohen Klippen handelt es sich um eine Kette aufeinanderfolgender weißer Kreidefelsen. Die weißen Kreidefelsen, die schroff vor dem blauen Meer abfallen – ein wahrhaft beeindruckender Anblick.

The coast between Eastbourne and Seaford in the south of England is designated as the “Seven Sisters”. With these impressive, tremendously high cliffs, it involves a chain of white chalk cliffs. The white chalk cliffs that drop off steeply before the blue sea – a truly impressive sight.

Grünes Gras, blaues Meer, weiße Felsen – kein Wunder, dass die malerischen Klippen Seven Sisters in Südengland bereits mehrfach als spektakuläre Filmkulisse dienten. Die Kreidefelsen erstrahlen in blütenweißem Gewand und bieten von oben einen schier atemberaubenden Ausblick auf das tosende Meer.

Green grass, blue sea, white rocks – no wonder that the picturesque Seven Sisters cliffs in southern England have already been repeatedly used as a spectacular film setting. The chalk cliffs shimmer in blossom-white garments and from above offer an almost breathtaking view of the raging sea.

Die „Sieben Schwestern“ thronen schon seit vielen Jahrhunderten über der Südküste Englands. Die Bezeichnung ist bereits um 1600 entstanden. Durch kontinuierliche Erosion hat sich nachträglich eine weitere Erhebung gebildet, so dass es heute eigentlich acht Schwestern sind. Die historische Bezeichnung ist jedoch erhalten geblieben.

The "Seven Sisters" have already reigned over the south coast of England for many centuries. The name arose as early as about 1600. As a result of continuous erosion, a further rise has subsequently been formed, so that today they are in fact Eight Sisters. However, the historical name has been retained.

Der dramatischste Strand
The most dramatic beach

Reynisfjara Beach/Island

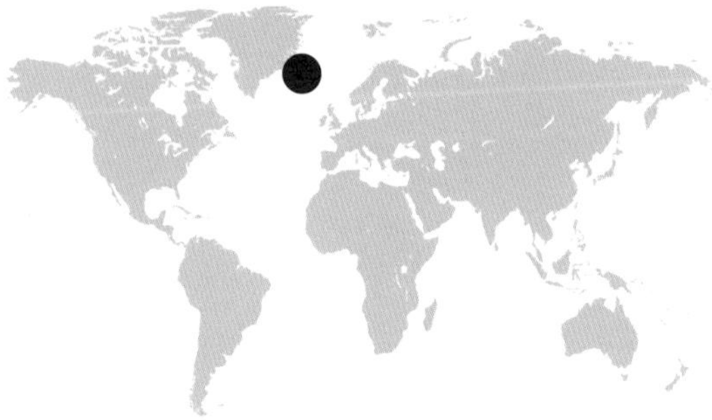

Der Reynisfjara-Strand an der Südküste Islands ist berühmt für seinen schwarzen Sand. Es ist ein Ort unbändiger und dramatischer Schönheit, an dem die tosenden Wellen des Atlantiks mit ungezügelter Wucht auf den Strand schlagen. Die Reynisdrangar-Basaltsäulen bilden bizarre Felsformationen, um die sich so manche Mythen ranken.

Reynisfjara beach on the south coast of Iceland is famous for its black sand. A place of boundless and dramatic beauty where the raging waves of the Atlantic hit the beach with unrestrained violence. The Reynisdrangar basalt columns form bizarre rock formations which are surrounded by myths.

Der Strand mit dem reinsten Quarzsand
The beach with the purest quartz sand

Whitehaven Beach/Australien

Der Whitehaven Beach vor der Ostküste Australiens gilt mit seinem Quarzgehalt von fast 99 Prozent als einer der weißesten Strände der Welt. Der Sand zeichnet sich durch eine Puderzucker-Konsistenz aus und bildet mit dem türkisblauen Wasser einen wundervollen Kontrast. Ein traumhafter, oft menschenleerer Strand, der nur per Boot oder Wasserflugzeug zu erreichen ist.

With a quartz content of almost 99 percent, Whitehaven Beach off the east coast of Australia is considered one of the whitest beaches in the world,. The sand is characterized by an icing sugar consistency and forms a miraculous contrast with the turquoise-blue water. A marvelous beach which is often empty of people and which can only be reached by boat or float plane.

Der sieben Kilometer lange Sandstrand Whitehaven Beach an der Ostküste der australischen Whitsunday Island mit seinem kristallklaren Wasser und dem unfassbar weißen Sandstrand sollte auf jeder To-do-Liste derer stehen, die das Paradies auf Erden suchen.

The sandy Whitehaven Beach seven kilometers long on the east coast of the Australian Whitsunday Island, with its crystal-clear water and the unbelievably white sandy beach, should be on every to-do list of those looking for paradise on earth.

Der Strand mit der stärksten Biolumineszenz
The beach with the brightest bioluminescence

Jervis Bay/Australien

Das Naturphänomen wirkt faszinierend und surreal zugleich: Mikroorganismen, die durch Biolumineszenz Feinde irritieren wollen, bringen das Wasser zum Leuchten und bescheren dem Betrachter mehr als einen magischen Moment. Zu den Stränden, die durch das Meeresleuchten nachts noch atemberaubender werden, gehört der Jervis Bay in Australien.

The natural phenomenon has an effect which is fascinating and surreal at the same time: Microorganisms, whose aim is to irritate their enemies through bioluminescence, bring the water alive with light and provide more than one magic moment for the observer. Jervis Bay in Australia is one of the beaches which become even more breathtaking at night as a result of marine phosphorescence.

Der salzigste Strand
The saltiest beach
Dead Sea/Israel

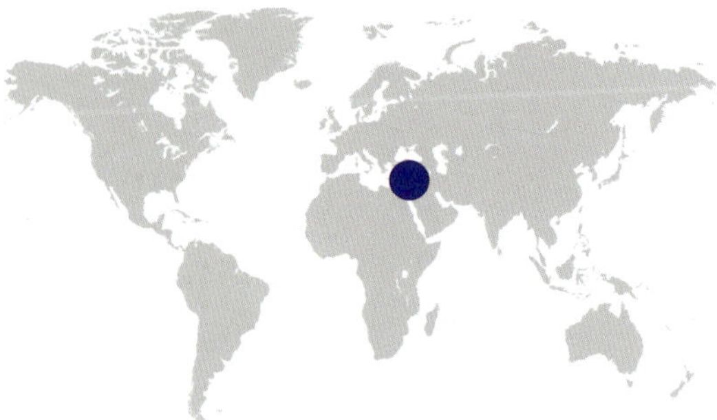

Das Tote Meer ist ein abflussloser See, der für seinen hohen Salzgehalt bekannt ist. Hier lässt sich – durch den enormen Salzgehalt – das Gefühl erleben, sich sicher vom Wasser tragen zu lassen. Das Baden im Toten Meer ist ein einzigartiges Vergnügen.

The Dead Sea is a lake which is not drained and which is known for its high level of salinity. Here you have feeling that you will be safely supported by the water – as a result of the enormously high level of salinity. Swimming in the Dead Sea is a unique pleasure.

Das Tote Meer an der Grenze zwischen Israel und Jordanien gehört zu den bekanntesten Reisezielen im Nahen Osten. Der Salzsee liegt inmitten einer bizarren Steinwüstenlandschaft mehr als 400 Meter unter dem Meeresspiegel.

The Dead sea, on the border between Israel and Jordan, is one of the best known destinations in the Middle East. The salt lake is located in the middle of a bizarre stony desert landscape, more than 400 meters below sea level.

Salzablagerungen zeichnen in Ufernähe faszinierende Formen. Mit Ausnahme von wenigen Algen und Bakterien kann durch die hohe Salzkonzentration kaum Leben im Wasser existieren, was dem See den Namen „Totes Meer“ verlieh.

Salt precipitation is characterized by fascinating shapes near the bank. Except for scant algae and bacteria, life can hardly exist as a result of the high salt concentration in the water, which has loaned the lake the name "Dead Sea".

Die Mineralien und Salze des Toten Meeres haben eine besondere Heilkraft und fördern die Gesundheit. Viele Arten von Hautkrankheiten können durch ein Bad im salzigen See gelindert werden.

The minerals and salts of the Dead Sea have a special curative power and promote health. Many types of skin illnesses can be eased by a bathe in the salty lake.

Der am schnellsten wachsende Strand
The fastest-growing beach

Lone Rock Beach/Lake Powell/USA

Ein freistehender Sandsteinfelsen, der Lone Rock, ist der Namensgeber eines der beliebtesten Strände in der Glen Canyon National Recreation Area. Durch zunehmendes Absinken des Wasserspiegels entstehen wunderschöne Sandstrände, wie der Lone Rock Beach.

A free standing sandstone rock, the Lone Rock, has given its name to one of the most popular beaches in the Glen Canyon National Recreation Area. Wonderful sandy beaches, such as the Lone Rock Beach, arise from the increasing drop of the water level.

Die mit den schroffsten Klippen gesäumten Strände
The beaches lined with the most precipitous cliffs

El Nido, Palawan and Tropical beach, El-Nido/Philippinen

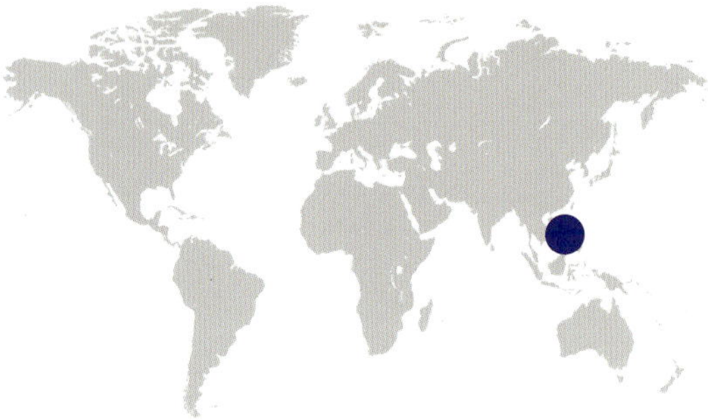

El Nido ist eine philippinische Gemeinde auf der Insel Palawan. Kalkfelsen ragen hier fast senkrecht aus dem Wasser und tragen zur besonderen Atmosphäre dieses Ortes bei. El Nido ist das Tor zum Bacuit-Archipel, Palawans größtem Naturparadies.

El Nido is a Philippine municipality on the island of Palawan. Limestone rocks jut out of the water almost vertically here and contribute to the special atmosphere of this location. El Nido is the gate to the Bacuit Archipelago and Palawan's greatest natural paradise.

Ein wahr gewordener Südseetraum: Weiße Strände, kristallklares Wasser, atemberaubend schöne Buchten und beeindruckende Korallenriffe machen El Nido nicht nur für Taucher zu einem wahren Paradies.

A south sea dream come true: White beaches, crystal-clear water, breathtakingly beautiful bays and impressive coral reefs, make El Nido a true paradise, and not only for divers.

Die bekanntesten künstlich angelegten Strände
The most famous artificial beaches

The Palm Jumeirah/Dubai

Wie eine riesige Palme ragt die künstlich angelegte Insel namens „The Palm Jumeirah" ins Meer. Dubais Küste ist durch diese ungewöhnliche Inselform um hundert Kilometer länger als zuvor. Mitnichten ein Projekt der Superlative.

Like a gigantic palm, the artificially-laid island by the name of "The Palm Jumeirah" juts out into the sea. As a result of this unusual island shape, the coast of Dubai is one hundred kilometers longer than before. Certainly a project of superlatives.

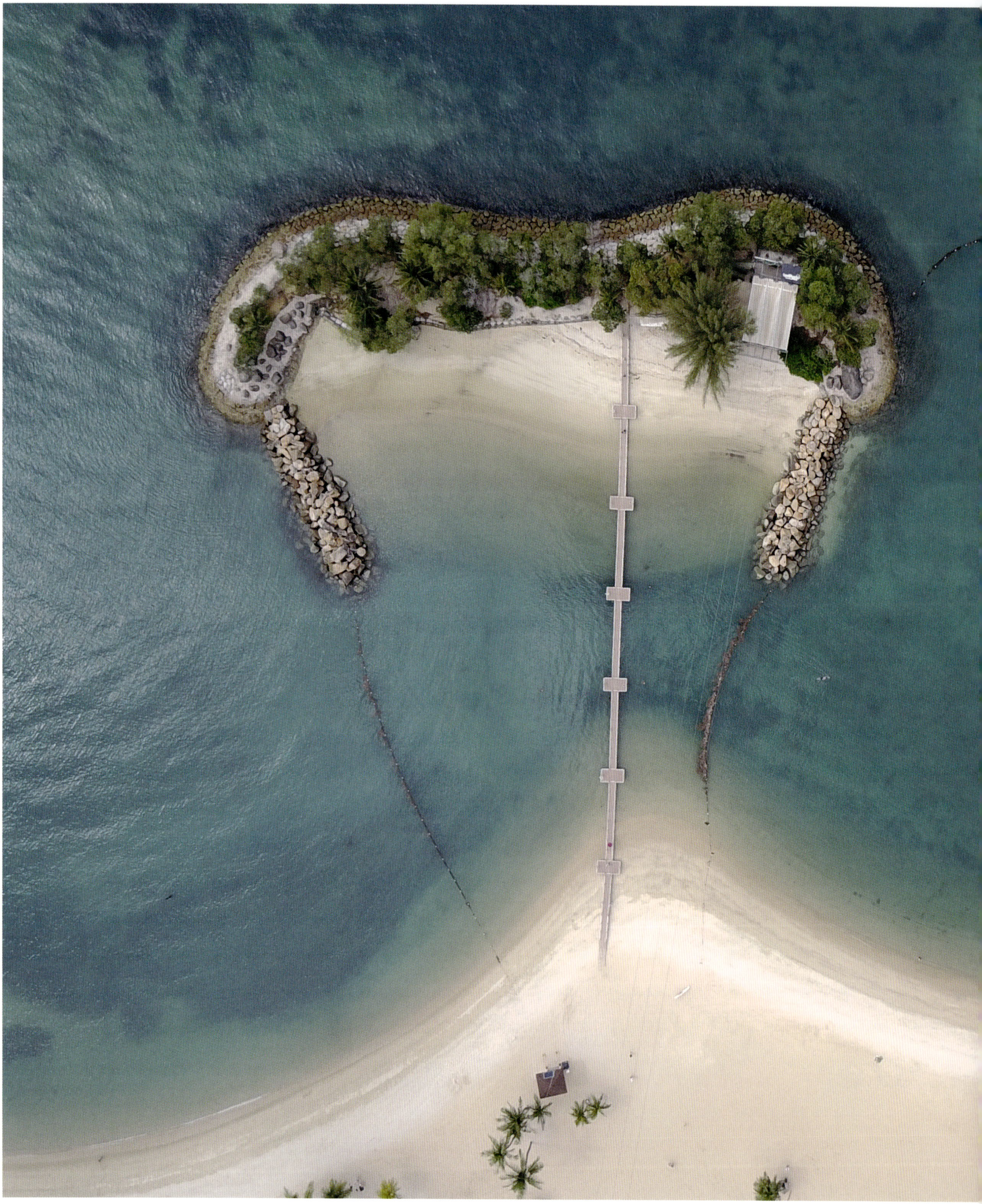

Sentosa Island/Singapore

Nur wenige Minuten von Singapur entfernt, lässt sich auf der nahegelegenen Insel Sentosa ein entspannter Tag am Strand einlegen. Die heutige Größe erreichte die Insel durch künstliche Landgewinnung. Durch Sandaufschüttung entstanden drei künstlich angelegte Strände, Palmen inklusive.

Only a few minutes from Singapore, a relaxing day can be spent on the beach on the closely sited island of Sentosa. The island has reached its present size through artificial land reclamation. Three artificially-laid beaches, including palms, have been formed from sand deposition.

Der rosaroteste Strand
The pinkest beach
Pink Sand Beach/Barbuda

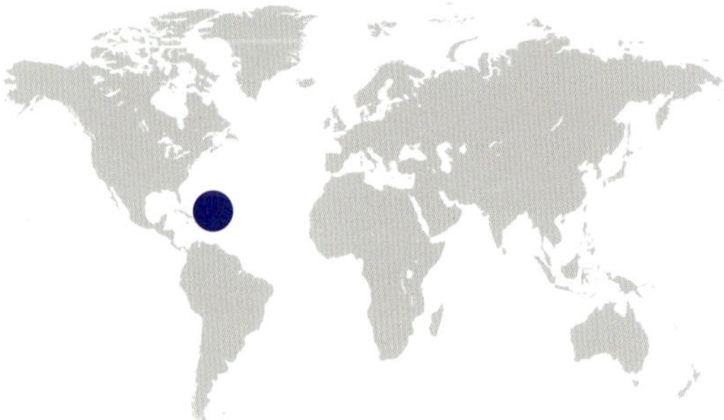

Es gibt Strände in vielen verschiedenen Farbtönen, aber Rosa ist wirklich exotisch. Dieser traumhafte Strand befindet sich auf der Insel Barbuda in der östlichen Karibik. Die Insel besitzt kilometerlange Sandstrände und viele vorgelagerte Riffe.

There are beaches in many different colors, but pink is really exotic. This marvelous beach is on the island of Barbuda in the eastern Caribbean. The island has miles of sandy beaches and many offshore reefs.

Der rosafarbene Farbton entsteht durch angespülte winzig kleine Teile von Korallen und Muscheln, die vom Korallenriff vor dem Strand stammen. Sie haben sich im Laufe der Zeit mit dem Sand vermengt und ihm den rosaroten Farbton verliehen.

The pink color arises from washed up tiny parts of coral and mussels, which come from the coral reef situated in front of the beach. With the passage of time, they have become mixed with the sand and this produces the pink-red color.

Der grünste Strand
The greenest beach

Papakolea Beach/Hawaii

Aus der Ferne sieht es aus wie eine saftige Wiese, so grün leuchtet der Papakolea Beach. Schuld an der grünen Farbe des Sandes hat ein Vulkan. Der Kegel besteht aus einem grünen Mineral, welches durch Erosion permanent an den Strand abgegeben wird.

Papakolea Beach lights up so green from a distance that it looks like a juicy meadow. The cause of the green color of the sand is a volcano. The cone consists of a green mineral, which is permanent deposited on the beach through erosion.

Unzählige Kristalle sind verantwortlich für die grüne Farbe des Strandes. Ewig wird der Strand nicht grün bleiben, denn das Olivin, welches die außergewöhnliche Färbung verursacht, wird im Laufe der Zeit ins Meer gespült.

Innumerable crystals are responsible for the green color of the beach. Eventually the beach will not remain green, because the olivine which causes the extraordinary coloring will be washed into the sea with time.

Der bunteste Strand
The most colorful beach
Glass Beach in Fort Bragg/Kalifornien

Unzählige bunte Glassteine: Was hier so faszinierend aussieht, ist tatsächlich durch jahrelange Ablagerung von Müll entstanden. Glas- und Keramikscherben wurden durch die Wellen nach und nach abgeschliffen und häuften sich schließlich am Ufer an.

The most colorful beach Glass Beach in Fort Bragg, California. Innumerable colored glass stones: What looks so fascinating here has in fact arisen from the deposition of garbage over years. Glass and ceramic fragments have been rubbed off little by little by the waves, and have finally accumulated on the bank.

Der Strand ist heute ein beliebtes Touristenziel. Die kunterbunten Glasscherben wurden vom Meer so rund geschliffen, dass es problemlos möglich ist, barfuß über die bunt schimmernden Glassteine zu laufen.

The beach is a popular tourist destination today. The motley items of broken glass have been worn round by the sea, so that it is possible to walk barefoot without any problem across the glass stones glimmering in many colors.

Der schönste Privatstrand Europas
The loveliest private beach in Europe

Spiaggia Rosa, Insel Budelli, Sardinien/Italien

Aufgrund von Schalenresten einer Koralle, die vor der Insel lebt, hat der Sand der kleinen Bucht Spiaggia Rosa eine pinke Farbgebung. Da viele Touristen den wertvollen Sand als Souvenir mitnahmen, ist der Zugang zum Strand für Urlauber inzwischen gesperrt.

Due to shell residues of a coral that is located in front of the island, the sand of the small bay Spiaggia has a pink coloring. Meanwhile, since many tourists take away the valuable sand as a souvenir, access to the beach has been blocked for holiday-makers.

Der überlaufenste Strand
The most crowded beach

Rimini/Italy

Urlaub könnte so schön sein, wenn da nur nicht so viele andere Menschen wären. Rimini, ein beliebter Badeort an der italienischen Adria, gehört im Sommer zu den Stränden, die ruhesuchende Urlauber besser meiden sollten.

Vacations would be so nice if only there were not so many other people around. Rimini, a popular bathing resort on the Italian Adriatic, is one such beach in the summer, which should better be avoided by holiday-makers looking for quiet.

Der schönste Strand an zwei sich vereinenden Ozeanen
The loveliest beach where two oceans meet

Cape of Good Hope/South Africa

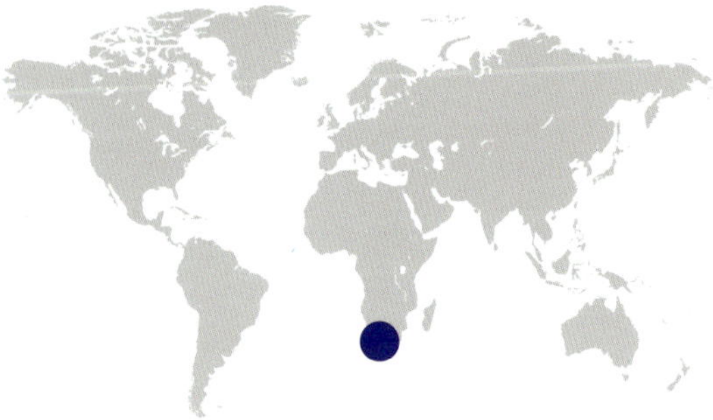

Das sagenumwobene Kap der guten Hoffnung ist eines der Highlights für viele Südafrika-Besucher. Belohnt werden sie mit einem atemberaubenden Blick von den 200 Meter hohen Klippen hinunter auf die tosenden Wellen. Über einen Wanderweg und Treppenstufen geht es hinab zu einem kleinen Sandstrand, dem Diaz Beach.

The legendary Cape of Good Hope is one the highlights for many visitors to South Africa. They are rewarded with breathtaking views of the raging waves from the 200 meter high cliffs. Via a hiking path and stairs, you can walk down to a small sandy beach, Diaz Beach.

Der schweinischste Strand
The piggiest beach
Out Islands, Exuma/Bahamas

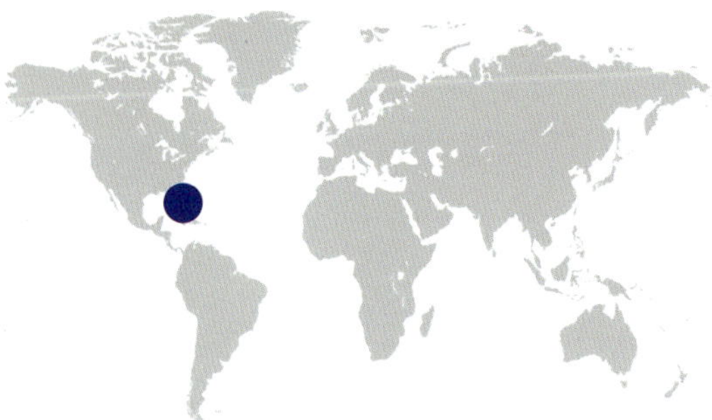

Traumhaft weiße Sandstrände, karibische Sonne, türkisblaues Meer und eine Horde gut gelaunter Schweine. Sie leben auf einer unbewohnten Insel namens Big Major Cay in den Out Islands der Bahamas.

Marvelously white sandy beaches, turquoise-blue sea and a herd of good-natured pigs, Caribbean sun. You live on an uninhabited island by the name of Big Major Cay in the Out Islands of the Bahamas.

Wer mag, kann eine Tour zu den niedlichen Schweinen buchen und mit ihnen eine Runde im kristallklaren Wasser schwimmen. Die schwimmenden Schweine auf den Bahamas sind mit Sicherheit ein einmaliges Erlebnis.

Whoever wishes can book a tour to visit the gentle pigs and swim around with them in the crystal-clear water. The swimming pigs on the Bahamas are certainly a unique experience.

Der affigste Strand
The beach with the most monkeys

Phi Phi Islands, Monkey Beach/Thailand

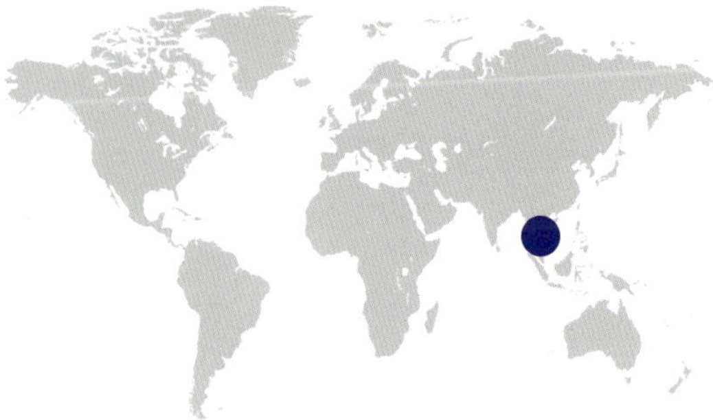

Der Strand hat seinen Namen den unzähligen Affen zu verdanken, die sich dort tummeln und sehr zutraulich sind. Die Affen lassen sich in freier Wildbahn und aus nächster Nähe beobachten.

The beach owes its name to the innumerable monkeys that romp there and are very trusting. The monkeys can be observed in free hunting grounds and at close proximity.

Der Strand mit den größten Wellen der Welt
The beach with the world's biggest waves

Nazaré/Portugal

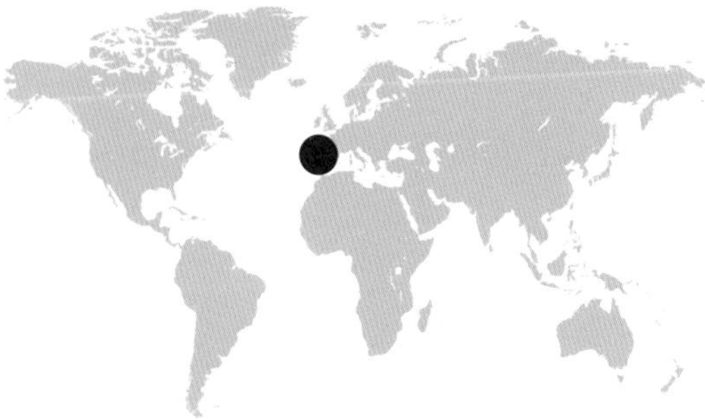

Die Big Waves haben Nazaré, ein kleines Fischerdorf an der Westküste Portugals, bekannt gemacht. Die Wellen können eine Höhe von 20 bis 30 Metern erreichen. Für abenteuerlustige Surfer geradezu die perfekte Welle.

Big Waves have made Nazaré, a small fishing village on the west coast of Portugal, well known. The waves can reach a height of 20 to 30 meters. For adventurous surfboarders, almost the perfect wave.

Der Wind peitscht, der Antlantik ist aufgewühlt, die Wellen bahnen sich mit brachialer Gewalt den Weg in Richtung Steilküste, grollen und brechen schließlich. Durch einen langen und tiefen Unterwassergraben vor der Küste entstehen hier die höchsten Wellen der Welt.

The wind lashes the Atlantic to fury, the waves clear a path with primitive power in the shelving coast direction, rise up and finally break. The highest waves in the world are formed from a long and deep underwater trench in front of the coast.

Der am meisten von Menschenhand geschützte Strand
The beach with the most man-made protection

Playa de Las Teresitas/Teneriffa

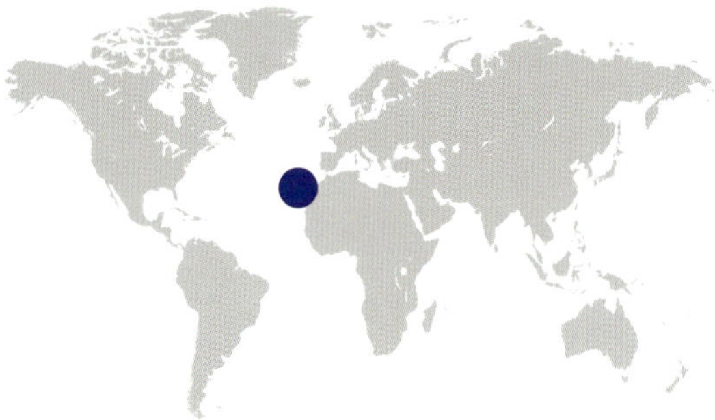

Der Playa de las Teresitas ist ein knapp zwei Kilometer langer Sandstrand. Auf den ursprünglichen schwarzen Sand wurde in den 1970er Jahren heller Sand aus der Sahara aufgeschüttet. Ein vorgelagerter Wellenbrecher soll vor der Erosion des Strandes schützen.

The Playa de las Teresitas is a sandy beach just two kilometers long. On the originally black sand, light-colored sand from the Sahara was deposited here in the 1970's. An offshore breakwater provides protection against erosion of the beach.

Der Strand mit dem schwarzesten Sand
The beach with the blackest sand

Reynisdrangar Rock and Reynisfjara Black Sand Beach/Island

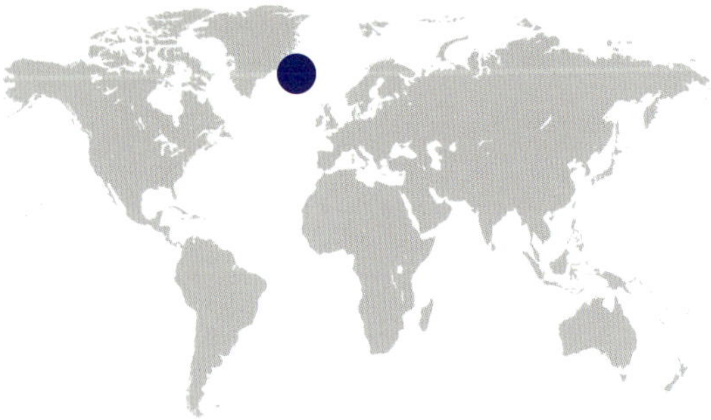

Die Reynisdrangar sind schwarze Felsnadeln, die fast bedrohlich aus dem Meer herausragen. Der Strand besteht aus pechschwarzem Vulkansand. Das Meer ist an dieser Stelle oft wild und aufgewühlt.

The Reynisdrangar are black rock needles which protrude almost alarmingly from the sea. The beach consists of pitch-black volcano sand. The sea at this location is often wild and rough.

Der Reynisfjara Beach an der Südküste der Insel ist der berühmteste schwarze Sandstrand in Island. Ein Besuch lohnt sich zu jeder Jahreszeit. Der mystische Ort entfaltet zu jeder Zeit eine unbeschreibliche Magie.

Reynisfjara Beach on the south coast of the island is the most famous black sandy beach in Iceland. A visit during all seasons is worth it. The mystic location unfolds an indescribable magic every time.

Die am ausfälligsten gerenderten Strände
The most strikingly rendered beaches

Wie würde ein Traumstrand aussehen, den man sich in seiner Fantasie so perfekt wie möglich ausmalt? Weißer Puderzuckersand, kristallklares Wasser, schattenspendende Palmen und vielleicht eine kleine Lagune – hier ließe es sich aushalten.

How would a dream beach look which one conjures up in fantasy to be as perfect as possible? White icing sugar sand, crystal-clear water, palms providing shade and maybe a small lagoon – this would be irresistible.

Meer- und Strandvisualisierungen zählen zu den begehrtesten Motiven, wenn man sich mittels einer Fototapete den Urlaub nach Hause holen möchte. Kein Wunder, können sie doch das Gefühl eines paradiesischen Urlaubsortes in die eigenen vier Wände zaubern.

Sea and beach views are among the most sought after motives if you want to bring the vacation back home by means of a photo collage. No miracle; you can conjure up the feeling of a paradise vacation spot within your own four walls.

Der mitreißendste Strand
The most breathtaking beach
St. Maarten/Netherlands

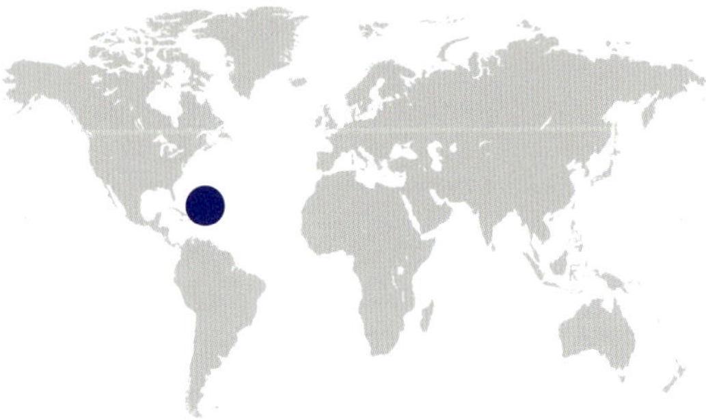

Er gilt als einer der berühmtesten Flughäfen der Welt – der Princess Juliana Airport im niederländischen Teil der Karibikinsel St. Maarten. Der Grund: Nur wenige Meter hinter der Landebahn beginnt bereits der Maho Beach. Während die Badegäste in der Sonne liegen, donnern nur knapp über ihren Köpfen die Flugzeuge hinweg.

It is considered as one of the most famous airports in the world – Princess Juliana Airport in the Dutch part of the Caribbean island of St. Maarten. The reason: The landing strip begins only a few meters behind Maho Beach. While the bathers are lazing in the sun the aircraft thunder by at almost head height.

HS-TKY

Flugzeugbegeisterte Besucher studieren extra die Flugpläne, um die großen ankommenden Maschinen live am Strand zu erleben. Ein nicht ganz ungefährlicher Nervenkitzel. Durch den Turbinenwind können Kräfte entstehen, die waghalsige Beobachter wegpusten und verletzen können.

Visitors who are aircraft enthusiasts study flight schedules separately in order to experience the large incoming aircraft on the beach. A not completely harmless thrill. Forces can arise from the turbine exhaust wind which can sweep away and injure daredevil observers.

Die weißesten Strände des hohen Nordens
The whitest beaches of the far north

Durness/Scotland

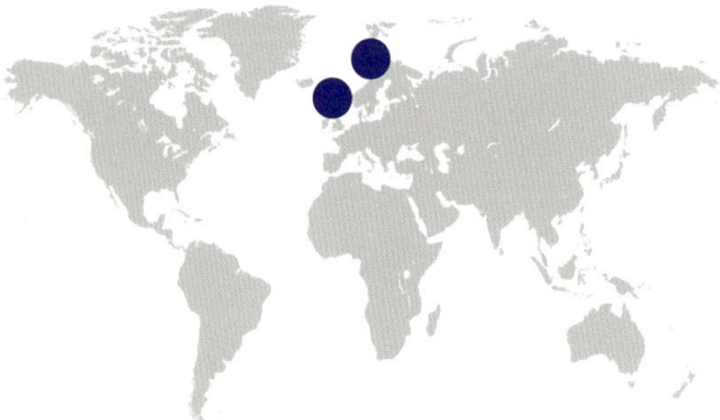

Durness/Scotland

Schottlands Norden verführt mit traumhaften Küsten. Geschwungene Buchten, gesäumt von saftig grünem Gras, auf dem Schafe weiden – hier lässt es sich vorzüglich entspannen. Das glasklare Wasser eignet sich aufgrund der kühlen Temperaturen zum Baden nur für Hartgesottene.

Scotland's north seduces with marvelous coastlines. Curved bays, bordered by juicy green grass where sheep graze – here is an excellent place to relax. Due to the cool temperatures, the crystal-clear water are suitable for swimming only for the hardest types.

Kvalvika Beach/Lofoten/Norway

Der Kvalvika-Strand liegt eingekesselt von den typisch lofotischen, rauen Bergen etwas abseits der Zivilisation. Es bedarf einer nicht wenig anstrengenden Wanderung, um den Strand zu erreichen. Die Mühe lohnt sich aber allemal, denn die Bucht ist ein absoluter Traum.

Kvalvika beach is cut off from civilization encircled by typically exotic, somewhat uneven, mountains. It requires strenuous hiking in order to reach the beach. The trouble is always worth taking, however, because the bay is an absolute dream.

Der muschelförmigste Strand
The most shell-shaped beach

La Rondinara/Corsica/France

Der muschelförmige Strand von La Rondinara liegt in einer wunderschönen Bucht umgeben von zwei Halbinseln. Feiner, weißer Sand, azurblaues Wasser, gesäumt von rötlichen Felsen wurde der Strand als schönster Strand Frankreichs klassifiziert.

The mussel-shaped beach of La Rondinara is located in a wonderful bay surrounded by two peninsulas. Fine, white sand, azure water, bordered by reddish rocks has resulted in the beach being classified as the most beautiful beach in France.

Der tödlichste Strand
The deadliest beach

Arromanches-les-Bains, Normandy/France

Ein Ort voller Geschichte: Bekannt geworden durch die Landung der Alliierten in der Normandie, erinnert heute nicht mehr viel an den Kriegsschauplatz von 1944. Die frühere Landungszone wird heute von Einheimischen und Touristen als normaler Badestrand genutzt.

A place full of history: Made known by the landing of the allies in Normandy, there is not a lot left that reminds one of the theatre of war in 1944. The former landing zone is used as a normal swimming beach today by locals and tourists.

Der versteckteste Strand
The most hidden beach

Hidden Beach/Mexico

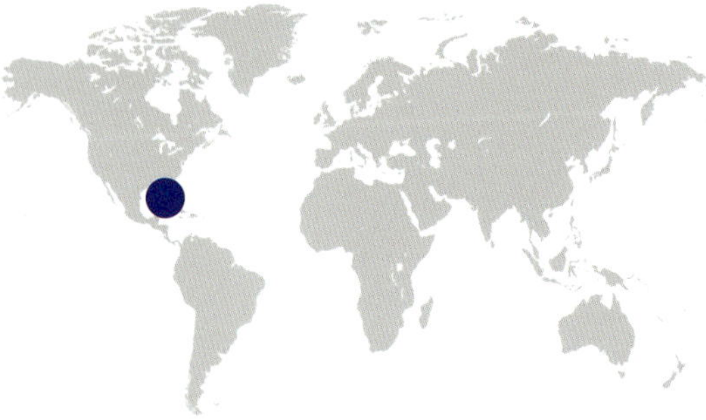

Vollkommen versteckt liegt der Hidden Beach in einem Loch auf einer unbewohnten Insel vor der Küste Mexikos. Erreicht werden kann der Strand nur durch einen mit Wasser gefüllten Felsentunnel. Aufgrund seiner Abgeschiedenheit trägt der Hidden Beach auch die Bezeichnung „Strand der Liebe".

The Hidden Beach is located completely hidden in a hole on an uninhabited island off the coast of Mexico. The beach can be reached only via a rock tunnel filled with water. Due to its seclusion, the Hidden Beach is also known as the "Beach of Love".

Bogengesäumte Strände
Arched-in beaches

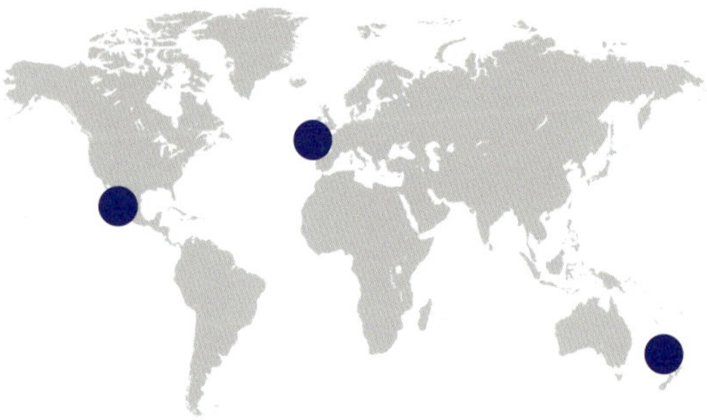

Cathedral Cove gehört ohne Zweifel zu den malerischsten Fleckchen auf der Coromandel Peninsula. Der natürlich entstandene Felsbogen ist ein allseits beliebtes Fotomotiv. Der Höhlendurchgang in einem Felsvorsprung verbindet zwei abgeschiedene Buchten miteinander.

Cathedral Cove is without doubt one of the most picturesque spots on the Coromandel Peninsula. The naturally-formed rock arch is a popular photographic motive for everybody. The cave passage in a rock ledge connects two separate bays with each other.

Cabo San Lucas, Mexico

Eine beeindruckende Felsformationen, die an der Südspitze der mexikanischen Halbinsel Baja California majestätisch aus dem Ozean emporragt, gilt bei Besuchern als beliebte Sehenswürdigkeit. Das Motiv des El Arco, ein natürlicher Felsbogen in den Meeresklippen, ist zu einem Wahrzeichen von Cabo San Lucas geworden.

An impressive rock formation, which rises majestically from the ocean at the southern tip of the Mexican peninsula Baja California, is a popular sight with visitors. The motive of the El Arco, a natural rock bend in the sea cliffs, has become a landmark of Cabo San Lucas.

Cathedral beach, Province of Lugo, Galicien, Spain

Der Kathedralenstrand gehört zu den spektakulärsten Stränden Spaniens. Bei Ebbe erheben sich dessen Felsen wie ein gotisches Gotteshaus aus dem Wasser. In der Nebensaison besteht die Chance, die magische Schönheit der Felsformationen ganz für sich allein genießen zu können.

Cathedral beach is one of the most spectacular beaches in Spain. At low tide, its rocks rise from the water like a Gothic place of worship. The opportunity to be able to completely enjoy the magic beauty of the rock formations for themselves only exists in the off season.

Der wegen eines Schiffswracks bekannteste Strand
The beach most famous for a shipwreck

Navagio Beach, Zakynthos/Greece

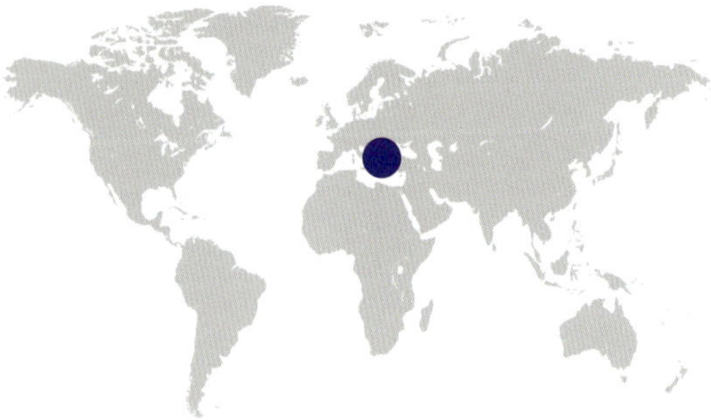

Meterhohe Felsen umschließen eine kleine, idyllische Bucht im Nordwesten der Insel Zakynthos. Das Highlight: Auf dem schneeweißen Sand liegt ein altes Schiffswrack. Auch als Schmugglerbucht bezeichnet, zählt das Kleinod mit dem glasklaren blauen Wasser zu den schönsten und außergewöhnlichsten Stränden in Griechenland.

Meter-high rocks enclose a small, idyllic bay in the northwest of the island of Zakynthos. The Highlight: An old shipwreck is located on the snow-white sand. Also designated as smuggler's bay, the jewel with the crystal-clear blue water is one of the most beautiful and most extraordinary beaches in Greece.

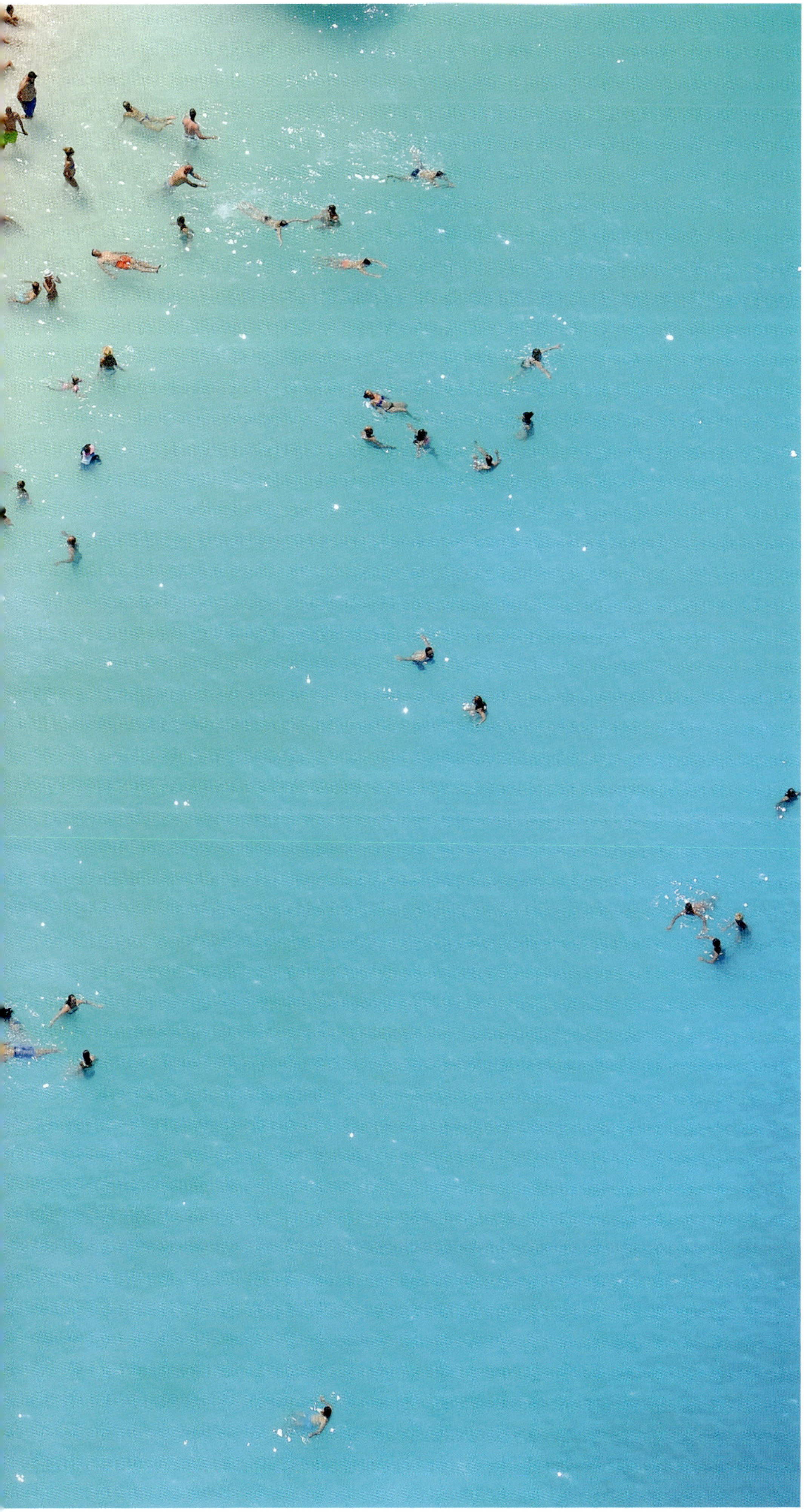

Das Wasser in der Region von Navagio hat einen einzigartigen azurblauen Farbton. Das kristallklare Wasser erlaubt Schnorchlern eine ausgezeichnete Sicht auf die Unterwasserwelt mit zahlreichen Mittelmeer-Fischen.

The water in the region of Navagio has a unique azure color. When snorkeling, the crystal-clear water allows an excellent view of the underwater world with numerous Mediterranean fish.

Durch die 200 Meter hohen Klippen, welche die Navagio-Bucht ringsum säumen, ist der Strand nur per Boot zu erreichen. Von der Aussichtsplattform über den Felsen eröffnet sich ein sensationelles Panorama über die traumhafte Bucht.

Due to the 200 meters high cliffs which border Navagio Bay everywhere, the beach can only be reached by boat. From the viewing platform above the rocks, a sensational panorama of the marvelous bay opens up.

Die berühmtesten Strände
The most famous beaches

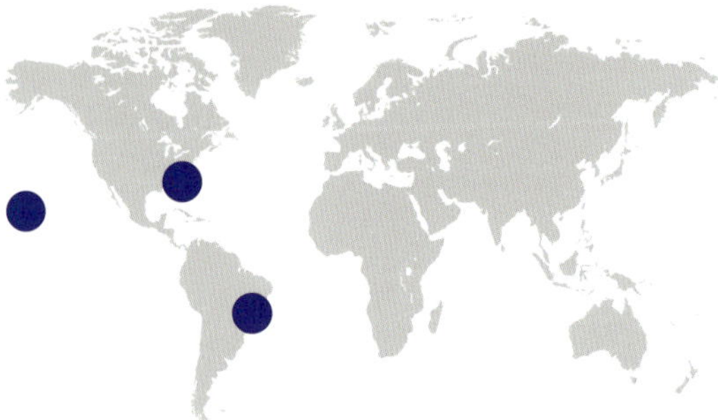

Copacabana, Rio de Janeiro, Brazil

Wer einen einsamen Strand sucht, ist hier mit Sicherheit an der falschen Adresse. Der vier Kilometer lange helle Sandstrand im Stadtteil Copacabana wird von Touristen und Einheimischen bevölkert. Die dahinterliegende Strandpromenade bietet jede Menge Unterhaltung in Form von Bars, Restaurants und Tanzlokalen.

Whoever is looking for a secluded beach has certainly not come to the correct address here. The four kilometers long, bright, sandy beach in the district of Copacabana is populated by tourists and locals. The linked promenade offers every form of catering in the form of bars, restaurants and dancing spots.

Ipanema Beach, Rio de Janeiro, Brazil

Sobald die Sonne langsam hinter dem Küstengebirge versinkt, zieht es die Einheimischen aus ganz Rio de Janeiro ans Meer. Tagsüber ein Paradies für Surfer und Sonnenbader, mausert sich der Ipanema Beach abends zum Spielfeld für hübsche Girls und muskelbepackte Männer.

As soon as the sun sinks slowly behind the coastal mountain range, the locals from the whole of Rio de Janeiro move to the sea. During the day a paradise for surfboarders and sunbathers, in the evening Ipanema Beach blossoms into a playground for pretty girls and muscle-building men.

Miami Beach, Florida, USA

Auf der vorgelagerten Insel Miami Beach finden sich einige der schönsten Strände Floridas. Sonnenschirme und Liegen sind an den meisten Stränden vorhanden. Das kristallblaue Wasser lädt zum vergnüglichen Baden ein. Dabei sollten jedoch immer die Fahnen der Lifeguards beachtet werden.

On the island offshore of Miami Beach are some of the most beautiful beaches in Florida. Parasols and recliners are available at most beaches. The crystal-blue water invites you to enjoyable swimming. However, the flags of the lifeguards should always be considered in this case.

Waikiki Beach, Honolulu, Hawaii

Waikiki Beach, an der Südküste der Insel Oahu gelegen, ist der am meisten besuchte Strand auf Hawaii. Der drei Kilometer lange Waikiki Beach ist gesäumt von Strandbars, Hotels und Restaurants. Am östlichen Teil des Strandes beginnen die ersten Ausläufer des Diamond Head, eine Tuffsteinformation und Wahrzeichen von Waikiki.

Waikiki Beach, the most visited beach on Hawaii, is located on the south coast of the island of Oahu. Waikiki Beach, which is three kilometers long, is bordered by beach bars, hotels and restaurants. At the eastern part of the beach begin the first spurs of Diamond Head, a tufa formation and landmark of Waikiki.

Der Strand an der engsten Bucht
The beach in the narrowest bay

Canal D'amour, Korfu/Greece

Felsen in beeindruckenden Formationen, dazwischen immer wieder kleine Buchten und Fjorde mit schmalen Sandstränden – einer davon ist der Canal D'amour. Namensgeber des Strandes war ein Felsentunnel im Meer. Verliebten, die gemeinsam durch den Tunnel schwammen, wurde ewige Liebe versprochen. Inzwischen ist der Tunnel eingestürzt.

Rocks in impressive formations and in between are found again and again small bays and fjords with narrow sandy beaches – one of these is the Canal D'amour. The name of the beach was bestowed by a rock tunnel into the sea. Eternal love was promised to amorous couples who swam through the tunnel together. Meanwhile the tunnel has caved in.

Auch ohne den Tunnel der Liebe lohnt sich ein Besuch des außergewöhnlichen Strandes. Die erosiven Kräfte von Wellen und Wind haben die hellen Sandstein- und Lehmfelsen im Laufe der Zeit in eindrucksvolle Formationen verwandelt.

Even without the tunnel of love, a visit to this extraordinary beach is worth it. The erosion forces of waves and wind have changed the bright sandstone and clay rocks over time into impressive formations.

Der eisigste Strand
The iciest beach
Jökulsárlón/Island

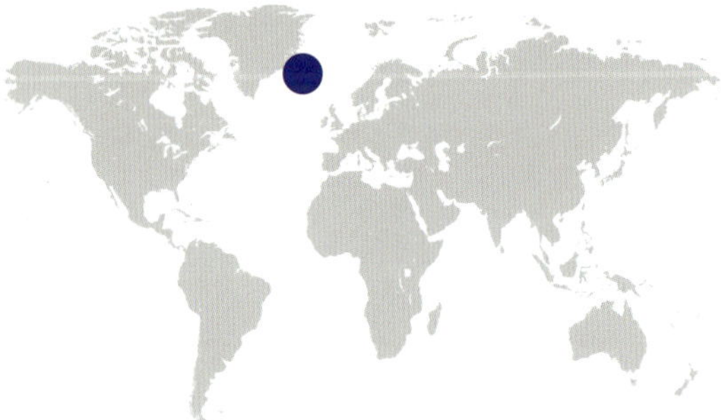

Die Gletscherlagune zählt zu den natürlichen Juwelen Islands. Die lupenreinen kleinen Eisblöcke auf dem schwarzen Sand des Diamond Beach erinnern an funkelnde Diamanten. Zweifelsohne ein Ort mit besonderer Magie.

The glacier lagoon is one of the natural jewels of Iceland. The microscopically-pure, small ice blocks on the black sand of the Diamond Beach remind you of sparkling diamonds. Without a doubt a location with special magic.

Das Eis stammt aus einer Gletscherzunge, die zur Lagune hinunterführt. Die Eisbrocken schmelzen langsam, treiben aufs Meer hinaus und werden von den Wellen zurück an den Strand gespült. Durch die permanente Veränderung sehen die Eisblöcke am Strand bei jedem Besuch anders aus.

The ice comes from a glacier which is sliding into the lagoon. The ice pieces melt slowly, move out into the sea and are washed back to the beach by the waves. As a result of the permanent change, the ice blocks look different with every visit to the beach.

Die klaren Eisblöcke auf dem schwarzen Vulkansand wirken bisweilen für den Betrachter surreal. Für viele Fotografen wird bei diesen faszinierenden Naturmotiven ein Traum wahr – insbesondere dann, wenn die Sonne scheint und zusammen mit den Eisblöcken für einzigartige Lichtreflexe sorgt

The clear ice blocks on the black volcanic sand occasionally strike the observer as surreal. For many photographers, these fascinating natural motives are a dream come true – in particular when the sun is shining and, together with the ice blocks, this guarantees unique light reflections..

Der muscheligste Strand
The beach with the most shells

Shell Beach/Australien

Dieser Strand besteht ausschließlich aus Muscheln. Der Shell Beach ist 40 Kilometer lang und Milliarden von strahlend weißen Herzmuscheln türmen sich zu einer bis zu zehn Meter dicken Schicht auf. Ein Paradies für Muschelsammler.

This beach consists exclusively of mussels. Shell Beach is 40 kilometers long and billions of shiningly white cockles are heaped up to form layers up to ten meters thick. A paradise for mussel collectors.

Die individuellsten Strände
The most individual beaches

Hot Water Beach/New Zealand

Der Hot Water Beach macht seinem Namen alle Ehre, denn hier sprudelt warmes Thermalwasser unter dem Sand hervor. Zwei Kilometer unter der Oberfläche befinden sich heiße Gesteinsschichten, die Reste vulkanischer Aktivität. Bei Ebbe steht das Wasser niedrig genug, um die heiße Quelle unter sich ausgraben und ein warmes Bad nehmen zu können.

Hot Water Beach honorably deserves its name because warm thermal water bubbles up under the sand here. Hot rock formations, the residues of volcanic activity, are located two kilometers below the surface. At low tide, the water level is low enough to enable digging up the hot source and taking a hot bath.

Einer der schönsten Doppelstrände
One of the loveliest double beaches

Porto Timoni Korfu/Greece

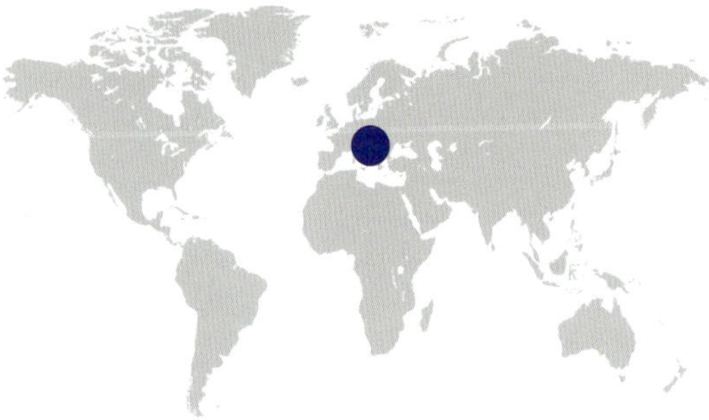

Unterhalb des Bergdorfes Afionas liegen etwas versteckt die bezaubernden Strände der Zwillingsbucht Porto Timoni. Ein schmaler Landstreifen trennt die beiden Strände voneinander. Die Besonderheit: Beide Strände haben eine unterschiedliche Wassertemperatur und unterscheiden sich in ihrer tiefblauen oder hellblauen Farbe.

Below the mountain village of Afionas are the enchanting beaches of the twin bay of Timoni, which are somewhat hidden. A narrow strip of land separates the two beaches from each other. Special feature: Both beaches have different water temperatures and differentiate in their dark-blue or light-blue color.

Der stinkendste Strand
The smelliest beach

Cape Cross/Skeleton Coast/Namibia

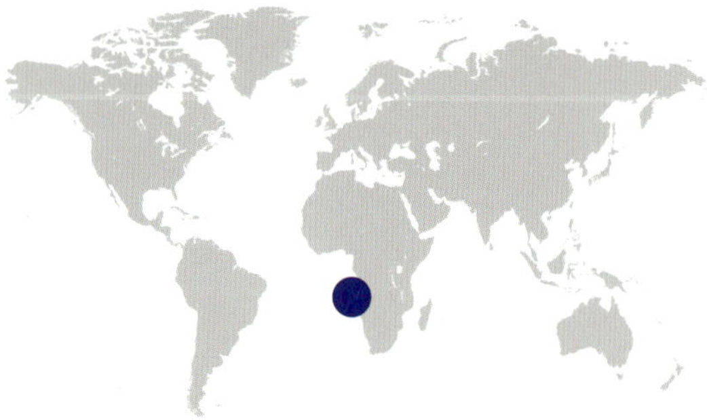

Cape Cross an der Skeleton Coast ist die Heimat der größten Seehundkolonien weltweit. Die Landzunge ragt tief in das Meer hinein. Die Fischgründe, welche die Robben mit Nahrung versorgen, sind entsprechend nah. Einziges Manko: der Gestank übelriechender Robbenexkremente.

Cape Cross on the Skeleton Coast is home to the largest seal colony in the world. The headland juts out deep into the sea. The fishing grounds which supply the seals with food are correspondingly close. The only shortcoming: The stink of smelly seal excreta

Der Strand mit der schönsten Kulisse
The beach with the most beautiful backdrop

Bora Bora/French Polynesia

Schneeweiße Strände, dazu das prächtige türkisblaue Farbenspiel der Lagune, im Hintergrund thront majestätisch der Mount Otemanu. Wasserbungalows sind auf Stelzen in die Lagune hineingebaut und bieten exklusiven Urlaub von der ersten bis zur letzten Minute.

Snow-white beaches and the splendid turquoise-blue play of color of the lagoon, crowned majestically in the background by Mount Otemanu. Water bungalows are built on stilts in the lagoon and offer an exclusive vacation from the first to the last minute.

Bora Bora zählt zu den exklusivsten und teuersten Reiseziel-en der Welt. Die luxuriösen Resorts in der traumhaften Lagune sind nicht grundlos das beliebteste Reiseziel für verliebte Honeymooner.

Bora Bora is one of the most exclusive and most expensive destinations in the world. Not without reason, these luxurious resorts in the marvelous lagoon are the most popular desti-nation for amorous honeymooners.

FOTONACHWEIS / PHOTO CREDITS

3 Cecilia Lim H M /shutterstock.com 4 Parshina Marina /shutterstock.com 6 Sven Hansche /shutterstock.com 9 SergiyN /shutterstock.com 10 emperorcosar /shutterstock.com 12 Oliver Le /shutterstock.com 15 Radek Borovka /shutterstock.com 16 Radek Borovka /shutterstock.com, 18 Radek Borovka / shutterstock.com, 21 Karl Ahnee / shutterstock.com, 23 weerasak saeku / shutterstock.com, 24 Ventura / shutterstock.com, 27 Nido Huebl / shutterstock.com, 29 paul prescott / shutterstock.com, 31 Tiam / shutterstock.com, 33 Andrey Bayda / shutterstock.com, 35 Hadrian / shutterstock.com, 37 ian woolcock / shutterstock.com, 39 Bertl123 / shutterstock.com, 41 Frank Fichtmueller / shutterstock.com, 43 Tanya Puntti / shutterstock.com, 44 Rachli Photos / shutterstock.com, 47 Jervis Bay Joanne Paquette 49 vvvita / shutterstock.com, 50 Kim Briers / shutterstock.com, 52 kavram / shutterstock.com, 54 vvvita / shutterstock.com, 57 blewulis / shutterstock.com, 59 R.M. Nunes / shutterstock.com, 60 Dmitry Pichugin / shutterstock.com, 63 Konstantin Stepanenko / shutterstock.com, 64 FuaadRCD / shutterstock.com, 67 BlueOrange Studio / shutterstock.com, 68 BlueOrange Studio / shutterstock.com, 71 Galina Barskaya / shutterstock.com, 72 Gary Gilardi / shutterstock.com, 74 Wollertz / shutterstock.com, 76 Aneta Waberska / shutterstock.com, 79 Mike Carballo / shutterstock.com, 81 Fishman64 / shutterstock.com, 83 alarico / shutterstock.com, 85 Miami2you / shutterstock.com, 86 BlueOrange Studio / shutterstock.com, 89 Anna Jedynak / shutterstock.com, 91 Albert Russ / shutterstock.com, 92 Bruno Aleixo Photo / shutterstock.com, 95 holbox / shutterstock.com, 97 Olga Gavrilova / shutterstock.com, 98 photosounds / shutterstock.com, 101 Mihai Maxim / shutterstock.com, 102 ixpert / shutterstock.com, 105 Chirawan Thaiprasansap / shutterstock.com, 106 Jaromir Chalabala / shutterstock.com, 109 Bildagentur Zoonar GmbH / shutterstock.com, 110 Lubomir Chudoba / shutterstock.com, 113 Samuel Borges Photography / shutterstock.com, 115 Bertl123 / shutterstock.com, 117 fernandocpauletto / shutterstock.com, 118 Dmitry Pichugin / shutterstock.com, 120 emperorcosar / shutterstock.com, 122 John_Walker / shutterstock.com, 125 Petr Kopka / shutterstock.com, 126 Calin Stan / shutterstock.com, 128 Ververidis Vasilis / shutterstock.com, 131 Catarina Belova / shutterstock.com, 132 R.M. Nunes / shutterstock.com, 134 Miami2you / shutterstock.com, 136 yuruphoto / shutterstock.com, 139 Calin Stan / shutterstock.com, 140 Calin Stan / shutterstock.com, 143 hofhauser / shutterstock.com, 144 ZinaidaSopina / shutterstock.com, 146 Dennis van de Water / shutterstock.com, 149 Marc Witte / shutterstock.com, 151 Fotos593 / shutterstock.com, 153 Calin Stan / shutterstock.com, 155 AgathaK / shutterstock.com, 157 wilar / shutterstock.com, 159 Martin Valigursky / shutterstock.com, 161 Mirelle / shutterstock.com, 162 Mirelle / shutterstock.com, 164 Mirelle / shutterstock.com.